A CRY FOR EDUCATION

A CRY FOR EDUCATION

Loreena Mary Minaudo

VANTAGE PRESS
New York

Certain names have been changed to protect the identities of the individuals portrayed herein.

Copyright © 1992, 1995 by Loreena Mary Minaudo

Published by Vantage Press, Inc.
516 West 34th Street, New York, New York 10001

Manufactured in the United States of America
ISBN: 0-533-11526-4

Library of Congress Catalog Card No.: 95-90303

0 9 8 7 6 5 4 3 2 1

I dedicate this book to my dad, Mario Minaudo, who died on December 12, 1985.

Like a Book, Know Me!

A book sits on a shelf,
its cover isn't appealing,
but you find yourself
staring at its title,
you become fascinated,
you pick it up, open it,
reading word by word,
sentence by sentence,
fascination becomes much deeper,
soon you are reading page by page,
chapter by chapter,
little by little you grow to love it.

Consider me the same way,
my handicap isn't appealing,
one might think it's an awful sight,
you might want to turn away from me,
but then you stop,
you realize that I am very bright,
my eyes tell you so,
along with my writings and my determination,
you may wonder where I came from,
you are fascinated with me,
but please beware,
like ice your heart may melt,
and you may fall madly in love with me.

Contents

Preface

My name is Loreena Mary Minaudo. I was born on a cold and dreary day, on March 3rd, 1953. I might not have survived my first week of life when my body then could not absorb sufficient oxygen, but by the grace of God, I did. Contrary to the nature of "normal" infants at their birth, my body functions could not utilize oxygen properly. The condition is the cause of my affliction, cerebral palsy—a handicap that renders the nerve endings of the central nervous system defective, so much so that muscle control is unstable, uncertain, and essentially uncontrollable.

If not for my affliction, I probably would not have an unusual story to tell, a story that reveals the truth about my academic education in a special educational classroom. Some teachers taught me, as well as the rest of their students, extremely well, while another taught us nothing.

A CRY FOR EDUCATION

Chapter One
My Therapy Days

One day, while thumbing through a magazine, I came across an article called "Educating Handicapped Children: 10 Years of PL 94-142." The title gripped my attention so much that I sat completely spellbound—as if it had some kind of hold on me. I forced my eyes downward to the first paragraph, which read:

> Ten years ago, Congress passed the Education for All Handicapped Children Act (PL 94-142), requiring the public schools to identify and then to provide special education services to youngsters with educational, developmental, emotional or physical disabilities. The law was hailed as a handicapped children's Bill of Rights, outlining a process whereby all children, regardless of the severity of their handicap, were to be assured the same educational rights and privileges according to their nonhandicapped peers—a free, appropriate public education.

Did I have a good education? I wondered. *Did my teachers have the qualificatons to open my mind? Were some teachers qualified to teach me, as well as other handicapped children?* Those questions fluttered in my mind, and soon I found myself drifting back in time. . . .

. . . *Was it so long ago that I sat among four hundred graduating students?* I wondered. It didn't seem possible that time had flown so quickly.

I remembered the evening of June 7th, 1972. In my

1

wheelchair, I was seated in the first row of graduates at the Light Guard Armory in Detroit, Michigan. The female graduates wore white gowns with white caps and red and black tassels, while the males wore blue caps and gowns.

The place was quite large. It was filled with lively, anticipatory chatter.

Oh, how well I do recall the feeling that I had as I sat there waiting for the graduation exercises to begin. I swallowed hard as a thousand butterflies swarmed inside my stomach. I was filled with mixed emotions, happy in one way that I was getting out of school for good, and in another sense, I felt quite sad, sad, for now my school days were ending. There was an emptiness like I'd never felt before. *Did I have a very good education in Mr. C's classroom?* I pondered, as I turned my head toward the audience.

My eyes swept the room, and after a few seconds, I spotted my brothers and their wives, my wonderful parents, and Mr. C, who had been my high school special education teacher. My dad's eyes locked into mine, and he proudly smiled. Oh, how delighted and proud he was of my accomplishments! I smiled warmly back, and then focused my eyes upon Mother, chatting with Mr. C, next to her. They both, in turn, looked at me and smiled.

The lights in the auditorium slowly began to dim, and I turned and looked directly at the stage before me. Instantly the air was filled with silence. A very handsome man walked out on stage and spoke to our class of 1972. He was U.S. Representative Donald Riegle. The speech was booed and hissed by many graduates, I recall. And even now I still remembered thinking how mean and insensitive they were. Maybe they were in a hurry to get home and didn't want to listen to anyone else from the "establishment." But I've come across people who don't want to listen to me. I deal with that each and every day of my life. No, I haven't been booed or hissed, but I must deal with people who don't want to listen to me because of my speech impediment. It's very hard for anyone to understand me unless they have the patience to really listen. No one was willing to listen to the congressman that evening and it must have hurt. I know it hurts me when I must deal with such insensitivity.

When the congressman walked off the stage, the principal of Lincoln High voiced enthusiastically, "Tonight we would like to congratulate the class of '72."

The whole audience cheered!!!

The principal waited awhile until the cheering had stopped and then announced, "We are now honored to present this diploma to a special student, a student who has been in a special educational classroom at Marjorie F. Carlson School. She typed all of her schoolwork on an electric typewriter. She is Loreena Minaudo!"

And at that very second, an eleventh grader from Lincoln High pushed me close to the stage. Cheers and claps filled the place as soon as the principal jumped off the stage and hurried over to me. Overjoyed, smiling from ear to ear, and with many uncontrollable arm movements, I shook his hand as he presented my diploma to me.

The eleventh grader started to push me back. It was then that I discovered that everyone was giving me a standing ovation. With tears streaming down my cheeks, I spotted Mr. C's face in the crowd and wondered if I deserved this diploma. *Do I, Mr. C?* I thought. Soon the clapping and the cheering slowly began to fade, and I began drifting back in time to when I was just a tot of three and a half years old. I remember that I sat, strapped to a chair, among physically challenged and retarded children, listening to a teacher who sat at a piano playing and singing "Eentsy Weentsy Spider."

Where's Mommy? Doesn't she love me anymore? Where am I? I thought, with bitter tears falling down my cheeks. I didn't know it at the time, but these questions were quite natural for any child who was attending her first day of school. However, I was much younger than children who started school at age five, the usual age, back in the 1950s. Of course, nowadays, in the 1990s, mothers send their children off to preschool at the ripe old age of three or earlier, but back then preschool was unheard of, to my parents anyway.

The reason that I attended the Detroit Orthopedic Clinic at such an early age was simple enough. It started on March 3rd, the day I fought my way out of my mother's womb. My parents named me Loreena Mary Minaudo. I weighed ten pounds and was twenty-four inches long. My mother, Jennie Minaudo, then age forty, and my father, Mario Minaudo, then age forty-eight, the proud parents, never thought that they would parent another child ten years after the birth of the last of their three sons. Their eldest son, John, was already married and had a two-month-old son of his own. Their son Joseph, then age sixteen, and their youngest son, Peter, then almost age ten, were healthy, normal schoolboys living happily at home. My parents owned a little neighborhood grocery store and toiled wearily, fourteen hours a day, seven days a week, to make a good living for their family. Unfortunately, accidents do happen, and I was theirs. A blessing or an unpleasant event? I do not know, nor did my parents at that time.

When I was born, I had to be placed into a hospital incubator because of breathing failure. So serious was my condition that the doctor gravely told my parents that I would not last the first night of my birth. The doctor, in fact, arranged for a Catholic priest to come and give me final blessings and they were administered to me that night. Three days went by and I was still alive, and the doctor and my parents were grateful that I was surviving.

As soon as I was able to breathe on my own, the doctor

had me removed from the incubator and had a nurse bring me to my mother. As my mother held me in her warm arms, she noticed that I had an unusual lump on the back of my neck.

"What is this lump doing on her neck?" Mother asked, worriedly.

"From the instruments used at her birth, but she's fine," the nurse reassured her. She added, "The doctor thinks you should feed her."

When my mother attempted to nurse me, I couldn't suck the sweet milk from her breast, and I began crying.

"There's something wrong with my baby," Mother cried.

"Let me bring her back to the nursery and have her bottle fed. I will have the doctor check her again," the nurse said, as she took me from my mother's arms.

Immediately, I was bottle fed and examined by the doctor who found nothing wrong with me. Later that day, he reassured my mother that I was fine. He simply prescribed cocoa butter to be applied to the lump that my mother had observed on the back of my neck. It was not then known that my inability to absorb oxygen had resulted in brain damage.

In a matter of days, Mother and I were released from the hospital and became immersed in our daily lives. Mother and Dad toiled away the hours in their grocery store, while I did what all babies do, slept, cried, cooed, and smiled. With the aid of cocoa butter, the strange lump that was on my neck, which had worried my mother, simply disappeared.

However, when I was seven months old, my parents began to suspect that I had a serious physical disability, for I was unable to support myself well in a sitting position. Horrified, my mother consulted our doctor, who referred my case to a nurse from the Visiting Nurse Association. Her name was Mrs. Fish.

It took several weeks after my mother's consultation

with the doctor for my mother's anxiously awaited visitor to ring our doorbell. Mrs. Fish appeared impressively capable and very businesslike as she politely identified herself to my mother. In my mother's gracious manner, she invited the nurse into the house.

"Please excuse me," Mother said, "the baby is taking a nap. I'll go and get her."

"Where's your kitchen?" asked Mrs. Fish. "I must use your kitchen table to examine the child on it."

Instantly, Mother pointed to our kitchen.

When my mother carried me into the kitchen, Mrs. Fish was now garbed in a white coat, the traditional uniform of the medical profession. Immediately, I was laid upon the cold and hard kitchen table, whereupon I was examined briefly by Mrs. Fish. She then turned toward my mother with a worried frown upon her face, as if she were about to divulge the most serious confidence.

"What's wrong with my baby?" Mother asked in a horrified voice.

In a quiet, articulate, and serious manner of voice, Mrs. Fish answered, "Mrs. Minaudo, Loreena has cerebral palsy."

"What is cerebral palsy?" Mother asked, quite puzzled.

"Cerebral palsy is a form of paralysis caused by injury to the brain from lack of oxygen at birth."

My mother's face turned pale, and her heart pounded rapidly. She didn't fully understand what cerebral palsy was, for back in those days, she hadn't seen anyone with this type of affliction, mainly because the handicapped were hidden away and never mentioned. Mrs. Fish reached out for my mother's hand and held it in comfort as they both stood in foreboding silence.

Despite the shock and confusion of the moment, my mother began to think back to the time when she had given birth to me and understood better. The birth had been a very,

very hard one. She, a forty-year-old woman, was in labor for twelve hours, and by the time she went into the delivery room, she had no strength to push. Instead of the doctor taking me from my mother's womb by means of a Caesarean section, he'd used forceps—grabbing me by my neck and forcing me out. If this method were used today, many doctors would be sued!

The suddenness and unexpectedness of Mrs. Fish' disclosure was too much for my mother. Even though she later prodded Mrs. Fish with many questions, Mother still continued to be bewildered. When Mrs. Fish left, my mother wanted a second opinion. Quickly, she phoned our doctor, who referred us to an orthopedic specialist by the name of Dr. Lay.

"How long do cerebral palsy victims live?" Mother asked Dr. Lay on the appointment day.

Dr. Lay, a very distinguished looking man, compassionately said, "As long as you or I."

"Can you tell me more about cerebral palsy victims?"

"It's hard to, Mrs. Minaudo, for all cases are different. Some have speech impairments, while others may not. Some may have walking difficulties. Loreena is much too young to tell. All that I can say is that these children get better with age and by having therapy," Dr. Lay explained.

My mother asked many more questions of the doctor, and he answered every one of them patiently and clearly, which left my mother with a fuller understanding of what cerebral palsy is.

And so, due to my handicap, I was attending my first day of school. Through my tears, I became intrigued with the contents of the room much more than singing and started to look around. It was an enormously large schoolroom, filled with a number of round table tops and chairs. A huge, almost walk-in size dollhouse with a red door and roof stood in the middle of the room.

Then I noticed an archway leading into a large room, and as my eyes glanced through it, I saw two women. A pleasant-looking black lady with a lovely smile, lovely enough to make anyone feel joyous, was assisting a little handicapped girl to walk. The other lady was giving kicking exercises to a little boy as he lay upon a big, red gymnasium mat. I watched the black lady therapist carry the little handicapped girl back to our classroom and sit her next to me.

"Such big tears," she said as she turned toward me. She then reached into her pocket, pulled out a Kleenex, and gently wiped the tears from my face.

"My name is Mrs. Bone, and I am your therapist. Would you like to come with me for a while for some exercises?"

Because of my shyness, and since I didn't know what was going to happen next, I just began weeping all over again.

Quickly, Mrs. Bone untied me from the chair, for my muscles still could not support me in a sitting position. She lifted me up in her arms and carried me into the therapy room. Once there, Mrs. Bone laid me down upon the big, red gymnasium mat.

"Loreena, can you spread your legs apart, like this?" she asked as she demonstrated on me what she meant.

At that stage of my life, I was pretty much a complete vegetable. I had a bright mind in a useless body. My body was so impaired that I could not yet crawl, feed myself, or do any of the other functions that a "normal" healthy three-and-a-half-year-old child would do. In other words, I was still being taken care of like an infant. My mother or father would feed, dress, and bathe me. So when Mrs. Bone asked me to spread my legs apart, I just lay there motionless. For the next half hour, I felt like a piece of bread dough. Mrs. Bone gave my body the workout of a lifetime! She stretched my arms and legs, gave me kicking exercises, and rocked me back and forth like a seesaw.

When Mrs. Bone brought me back to my classroom, Ms. Moody was seated at a large, round table with many children around her.

"Please, seat her next to me," Ms. Moody said to Mrs. Bone. The therapist nodded and I was then seated upon a chair, and once again she tied me to it.

Once seated at the table, I noticed Ms. Moody showing each of us how to construct a puzzle. She pulled apart its five attractively colored wood pieces, consisting of a yellow banana, a green pear, a red apple, an orange-colored orange, and a bunch of purple grapes. Then she asked us, one at a time, to put the pieces back together again. Some achieved this goal readily, while others were too severely retarded to perform this simple task. When it became my turn to construct the fruit puzzle, I pointed with uncontrollable and unstable movements of my left arm to the piece of fruit that belonged in each slot, and Ms. Moody would place the pieces where I directed.

Later that day I was given my first speech lesson with a speech therapist by the name of Miss Sand.

"Loreena, will you repeat after me?"

Before I had a chance to answer the question, she slowly and clearly, exaggeratedly, enunciated, "A-A, E-E, I-I, O-O, U-U," and I repeated them back to her the best I could in my garbled speech pattern. Continual repetition persisted under her direction for some time. Then she placed a small quantity of peanut butter on my upper lip and instructed me to lick it off with my tongue. My attempts were unsuccessful, though I tried and tried.

The last therapist on my first day of school was an occupational therapist by the name of Mrs. L. At a table she put some blocks in front of me and instructed me to watch carefully while she placed one block on top of another. Next, Mrs. L. disassembled the blocks and asked me to do what she had done. Due to tremendous overflow of movement in my hands and arms, the task of even grabbing onto a block was useless, let alone placing one block on top of another.

Seeing this, Mrs. L. insisted that we play a little game. Actually, she wanted to see how good my coordination was and tested it by asking me to touch, with a finger of my left hand, my mouth, nose, eye, ear, etc. She watched carefully as I struggled to do so. Next, she instructed me to do the same with my right hand, and, of course, I did.

When the thirty-minute session had ended, Mrs. L. carried me back to the classroom. I knew that the day had ended, for the children were donning their sweaters. For the first time all day, I smiled. I realized that I was going home to see the lady I'd missed all day—my mother. This was surely a memorable day—my first day away from home, filled with much fear, bewilderment, and confusion. I had had enough!

Unlike the first day of school when I cried for my mother, in the days, weeks, and months that followed, I grew to love going to the Detroit Orthopedic Clinic and being with such devoted therapists as Miss Sand, Mrs. Bone, and Mrs. L. Each therapy session brought new hope into my bleak life. Even though my progress was slow, my therapists were determined to train my body to function as normally as possible.

I will now give you three examples of what these three devoted therapists did to enrich my life.

One afternoon, while a helper-aide was feeding me a hot lunch from a tray, Mrs. L. appeared from out of the blue. She startled me, and I jumped. "Sorry, hon. Didn't mean to scare you," the therapist sweetly said as she stood there, watching me being fed.

"Can she hold the spoon?"

The helper-aide shook her head no and added, "But she is able to grab bread in her hand and eat it. See?" She then broke off a piece of bread and placed it in my left hand. Mrs. L. observed as I began to eat the bread for a few seconds. Then she turned and left the room.

The next time I was in the occupational room, Mrs. L. put in front of me a sticky placemat on which she set a plate and spoon. The purpose of the sticky placemat was to keep the plate from sliding. I watched closely as she opened a can of chocolate pudding and scooped out a few spoonfuls onto the plate. Then she tied a bib around my neck and put the spoon in my right hand, which she repeatedly guided with hers down to the plate and up to my mouth.

After ten minutes, she released her hand from mine so that I could try independently, and try I did. Flying pudding droplets went everywhere, on the floor, in my hair, nose, etc.—everywhere but my mouth! But even as young as I was, I did not become discouraged and just tried again and again.

Yet during that occupational therapy session, all of my attempts to feed myself were unsuccessful. For days and weeks, repeats of it continued! Then, one day, it happened! I fed a spoonful of chocolate pudding into my mouth, and I smiled.

"I knew it! I knew you could feed yourself!" Mrs. L. cheered as she placed a gentle kiss on my forehead. And so, from that day forward, due to this devoted therapist, I learned to feed myself. Learning to eat without aid from anyone was indeed a difficult project for me and a real accomplishment. Likewise, learning to drink through a straw was an equally difficult task.

I was a tot of four when Miss Sand tried to get me to drink through a straw. She tried for months! With the straw in between my lips, in a glass of cold water, I would just sit in speech class, completely baffled, every time she instructed me to "suck." It was a word that I just couldn't comprehend. When all attempts failed, Miss Sand confided in a phone conversation to my mother my failure to drink through a straw. She encouraged my mother to practice the task with me at home, where she thought I might respond much better.

One Saturday morning, Mother decided to tackle the task. She sat me in my highchair and pushed me close to the kitchen table. Mother turned and walked over to the sink, where she filled a glass with cold water and placed a straw into it.

As I sat there waiting for her to bring me the glass, I remember the kitchen smelling of Italian biscuits that were baking in the oven. Mother called them biscuits, but they were really like cookies and the aroma made my mouth water. I watched as she lowered the oven's heat before she brought the glass over to me. The thought of practicing made me queasy because I knew I couldn't do it. I would much rather have had one of those biscuits.

And for the hundredth time, I did what I always did. Just sat there with the straw in between my lips, not sucking. "Ma, I'm hungry. Will you fry me a hamburger?" my brother Peter whined, as he walked into the kitchen. "Just chased Michael and Gary around the block."

The second that Peter mentioned the two boys' names, I pulled away from the straw and my eyes opened wide.

"Keep practicing, Loreena," Mother said as she went over to the freezer to get a hamburger and then plopped it into the frying pan. As if Mother could read my mind, she added, "They will be here shortly to play with you, don't worry!"

I smiled and placed the straw between my lips once again. Michael and Gary were my two nephews. Yet back then, they were like brothers to me.

While Peter poured himself a glass of cold milk, he

noticed me sitting at the table with a glass of water and the straw in my mouth, not sucking. "What is Sis doing?" Peter asked.

"I'm trying to teach her how to drink from a straw, but she isn't responding," Mother answered, discouraged, as she took the Italian biscuits out of the oven. I wanted one.

Peter then sat down at the table across from me, drinking his milk and observing my efforts to drink from the straw.

Peter was a tall, thin kid of fourteen. He had dark brown hair and eyes. His cheeks were always rosy. He was the youngest of my three brothers. Since there were ten years between us, I really didn't see him that much, except for meals.

Suddenly, the kitchen grew completely quiet. All that could be heard was the hamburger sizzling in the frying pan. Finally, Peter said, "Loreena, kiss the straw. Go on, kiss it!"

I looked up at Peter and giggled. I thought he was just teasing me.

"Hey, c'mon now!" he shouted. "I'm trying to help you. Kiss the straw!"

So, with that, I obeyed Peter's command. At first when I kissed the straw, the water came up just a tad and instantly went back down again.

"Give a bigger kiss, Sis."

Once again, I tried and the water came halfway up the straw and then went back down again. As I struggled, I suddenly heard running footsteps coming into our kitchen.

"Grandma!" Gary said happily as he ran over to my mother and kissed her.

"Hi, Grandma and Uncle Peter," Michael greeted them.

"Hooray, Reenie is home. Reenie," Gary greeted me, running over to me. Reenie is my nephew's nickname for me.

"Hold it, boys. We're doing something here," Peter said.

"Here, boys, have a hot biscuit while you watch Uncle

Peter teach Reenie how to drink from a straw," Mother said, taking the hamburger out of the frying pan.

"Mmmm, thanks!" the two boys shouted in unison.

I kissed the straw hard, and to my surprise I tasted a drop of cool water. Overjoyed, I kissed, and kissed, and kissed—each time tasting water.

"You're doing it, Sis," Peter said proudly.

"She sure is!" Mother cheered.

"Reenie is drinking," Michael said.

"Can we play with Reenie now?" Gary asked his grandmother.

"Sure."

Mother asked, in an amazed tone of voice, "Peter, how in the world did you come up with that great idea when the speech therapist, with a college degree, couldn't?"

Peter just shrugged.

Having daily physical therapy sessions with Mrs. Bone turned my useless body into a workable one. Even though my progress was slow, she taught me how to crawl on my hands and knees. She taught me by placing me, belly down, on a big beach ball. Behind me, Mrs. Bone would then push my feet, one at a time, until I could get the hang of it. Then she would let go, and I would try. At first I couldn't, but then, after six months or so, I mastered the task of crawling.

After Mrs. Bone taught me how to crawl, she taught me how to stand and to walk with an aid of a walker. I am most thankful to Mrs. Bone for this, for I am still walking with the aid of a walker.

Now that I have reflected on my therapy days, I feel such a need to nit-pick on a handful of events that happened during these days. I must state clearly here that I hope I don't come off as a Miss Know-It-All. Believe me, I am not! But I do feel that I have a right to freedom of speech. Our Constitution says so. The opinions that I will express in the following paragraphs are truly mine and mine alone. Others may not like what I am going to reveal; yet I hope some parents of physically challenged children, doctors, nurses, and anyone in the special education field will find this useful and insightful.

Oh, what sweet memories I have of Mrs. Bone. I can still feel her gentle hands upon my body as she would exercise my legs and arms. I felt like a piece of bread dough as she exercised my limbs. I was, like all tots, sometimes tired and cranky. I wasn't always in the mood for therapy, even though therapy was a must—an absolute necessity. The very lovely physical therapist found her own solution in dealing with recalcitrant children. Mrs. Bone would use the distraction method. She would sing or play games with the little child while she would give him/her exercises.

I also remember a certain rhyme that Mrs. Bone would recite rhythmically as she would spread my legs apart and close them again, like a pair of scissors. "One, two, buckle my shoe. Three, four, close the door. Five, six, pick up sticks. . . . "

A smile would spread across my face from ear to ear as I listened quite intently. I thought it was a neat but silly rhyme, and at times I would even let out a few giggles. Thanks to this distraction used by this wonderful therapist, I would forget all about being tired and that I was doing exercises.

There were times when Mrs. Bone would encourage me, saying, "Come on, hon. Repeat after me. I know you can."

Unfortunately, at that stage of my life I did not obey. I just listened to the words to the rhyme as I took in the contents of the therapy room, where tricycles, walkers, and crutches hung on the walls. I never spoke much. Not even holophrases (one-word sentences). I had always gotten my needs met by pointing to the things I wanted. For instance, if I wanted a cookie, I would point to the cookie jar and my mother would instantly give me one. However, during my second year of life, Mother put an end to my pointing.

One evening, she sat me in my little, wooden rocking chair and tied me to it so that I wouldn't fall off. "Here, play with Freddy while I wash the dinner dishes," she said, as she placed a brown plush teddy bear on my lap.

I smiled down at my cute teddy bear, and we both started to send telepathic messages to one another. This was how I played inside my useless body. I was much too young to comprehend that my bodily efforts were usually fruitless.

After a while my throat felt very parched and, with extreme, uncontrollable, and unstable movements of my left arm, I pointed a closed, clenched fist toward the faucet. I then let out an unnatural groan! This was my way of alerting Mother that I wanted a drink of water.

She looked to see what I wanted, but this time she did not move. She just stood at the kitchen sink washing the dinner dishes, avoiding me completely. In my natural way, I once again groaned. Still no response from my mother. I grew furious and started to cry.

"Go on and cry," Mother yelled, "but you aren't going to get any water until you say it! Say 'water!' 'Wa-ter.' 'Waawa!' "

The sharpness of Mother's voice startled me, and I jumped. I wasn't used to such treatment coming from Mother.

"Say 'water.' 'Wa-ter!' 'Waawa,' Loreena!" Mother repeated.

I stopped crying and slowly garbled, "Waaaaaawaaa!"

"That's it! Say it again," Mother encouraged me.

"Waaaaaawaaa!"

Mother then filled a glass of cold water, walked over to me, stooped down, and held the glass up to my lips, while I drank. She said, "No more pointing, Loreena. From now on you must tell me what you want. Do you hear me?"

I nodded.

And so, my holophrases began. Unfortunately, I only spoke when I was at home—never at school and never to Mrs. Bone, who wanted me to repeat the rhyme after her. Every time I think about Mrs. Bone, I wonder how many physical therapists used, or are using, the distraction method on very young children. I am talking about children who are between the ages of two up to six, the ages when children are only interested in things for only a few minutes or so—children who lack patience!

Physically challenged children are the same as able-bodied children. We, too, get bored with things quite quickly. So could you imagine a child receiving a thirty-minute physical therapy session five days a week? It can be very monotonous! I truly recommend that all physical therapists play games with or recite rhymes to the child who is receiving therapy. Make the atmosphere as pleasant and as warm as possible.

I know that Mrs. Bone made quite an impression on my young life, an impression that is still imprinted in my heart and soul. She gave me warmth, and love—creating an atmosphere that was greatly needed; but most and above all, she worked on my vegetative body and gave it life!

Yes, it's true that I never talked when I was at school. Bear in mind that I was much too shy. But there was one person who wouldn't let me get away with it—Miss Sand, the speech teacher at the Detroit Orthopedic Clinic. Daily, I would have to repeat vowel sounds after her.

She was a fine therapist. I have no complaints when it comes down to repeating vowel sounds, or when we started to use holophrases, or complete, whole structured sentences. These are a necessity! However, when it comes down to other methods that the child can't do or won't even be able to do throughout her/his life, then stop the torture!

An example of this torture was when Miss Sand would smear peanut butter upon my upper lip and would then ask me to lick it off with my tongue. It was on these daily occurrences that I felt like a sheet of cookie dough being dressed in icing! Oh, how silly I must have looked! Yet I always did what I was told. I tried to, anyway. Oh, how hard I tried to lick the peanut butter off my upper lip, but my tongue was like a bear in hibernation not coming out to do its duty. I firmly believe that the therapist must practice with the child for a certain period of time, perhaps two months but not longer, to discern the capability of the child to accomplish a particular task.

Miss Sand did this certain exercise routinely for the two years that I was with her at the clinic. I know that she meant well. But my goodness, if a child can't do a certain exercise, then it is time to quit. It is time to stop frustrating the child! Another teaching method that I considered a waste of time was when Miss Sand would light a candle and expect me to blow it out. It was another technique that went on daily over the two years that I was at the Detroit Orthopedic Clinic. I couldn't blow then, and I still can't. So why keep on trying?

I did not know at that time that Mrs. L. would be the only occupational therapist I would have throughout my school days, with the exception of another therapist whom I had when I was in my last year of school. The schools that followed the Detroit Orthopedic Clinic never had an occupational therapist. Oh, they tried to employ one, but none would stay more than a week or two. Furthermore, except for Mrs. L., I was a puzzle to all the OTs who tried to work with me.

You see, almost all of the physically challenged children would use the right or left hand. I, however, can use both hands, but not very well and not simultaneously. For instance, when I eat a cookie, I will hold it in my left hand, and when I feed myself with a spoon or a fork, I use my right hand. This baffled the OTs. I never understood why and I still can't! It seems perfectly natural to me.

Yet Mrs. L. found no obstacles when she taught me how to feed myself. Always an optimist, she worked with me, as she did with any other physically challenged child, as an individual. She never asked why I used both hands. It was, and still is, my way.

A few months before I left the clinic, Mrs. L. taught me how to don a jacket. I am sad to report that it was the only piece of clothing with which she instructed me. Time was like a thief in the night, robbing me of more occupational therapy sessions with this fine person. Yet Mrs. L. instilled such optimism and determination deep in my soul that I became my own occupational therapist.

As I grew older, I would, and still do, buy easy-to-put-on clothing. No buttons, snaps, or hooks for me! My shorts and slacks all have elastic waistbands. My dresses, skirts, and blouses are all slip-ons. I also learned how to put my own lipstick, cook—somewhat—and other things that were and still are a real struggle for me to do.

In this first chapter, I have shared my experiences in my speech, occupational, and physical therapy sessions with such devoted therapists. However, I will not write any more about my therapy days in the following chapters. Readers may be wondering why. In honest truth, I feel that many books have been written on individuals that focus on their sessions . . . books such as *The Miracle Worker, Karen, Jody,* etc. But I feel a need to focus on my education in a special education classroom in order to enlighten parents of physically challenged children, special education instructors, and anyone else who is interested in "the right for a physically challenged child to have a good education."

Nevertheless, since the Detroit Orthopedic Clinic had been a part of my school days, I felt a need to write about the events that happened there and, please, take a word of advice. Send your physically challenged child to therapy sessions early in his/her life. It sure helps!

Chapter Two
The Chippendale Years

"C'mon sweetheart," Mr. Pitts said, as he gently lifted me out from his station wagon and, like a sack of potatoes, threw me over his broad left shoulder.

I giggled as he carried me into the school building. He was a tall and dashing young man, who always smoked a pipe and always reeked of tobacco. I do recall he was employed by the school district to drive handicapped children to school and then bring them back home again.

"Where do I put this special one?" Mr. Pitts asked a slim, attractive-looking teacher with curly auburn hair, who was seated at her desk.

"Let me see if she belongs to me," the teacher sweetly said, looking down at a list of names.

Mr. Pitts asked, "Are you Miss Glad?"

She nodded affirmatively.

"This little thing is Loreena Minaudo."

"She's mine, all right." She smiled, rose to her feet, and walked over to us. "Put her down by the round table."

I was just a tot of five-and-a-half years, and at that stage of my life, I didn't have any balance whatsoever. I couldn't walk, hold my head up, or sit in a chair properly. I remember that when Mr. Pitts sat me in a chair, a panicky feeling came over me. I was fearful of falling off the chair, and I burst out crying.

"It's okay, little one," she comforted as she picked me up in her arms and carried me over to her desk, where she got out a strap from one of the drawers. She then brought me back to the chair and strapped me into it. Now feeling secure, I smiled.

"I'm Miss Glad, your kindergarten teacher," she said as she took off my sweater. I watched as she helped other children with their sweaters. Even at that age, I was very observant and noticed that the children were handicapped. I was much too young to know what the devices were called that were worn by each child, only learning when I was older the names of devices such as hearing aids, artificial limbs, braces, walkers, etc.

On that first day of school at Chippendale, Miss Glad began by giving each student a puzzle to do. She watched closely while we did our puzzles—trying hard to see which children struggled the most and which the least. When it became my turn to construct the puzzle, I motioned with uncontrollable movements of my right hand to Miss Glad as she placed the pieces in their proper slots. She was quite amazed that I did it so quickly.

As in all kindergarten classes, we had a milk and cookies break, played games, learned a new song or two, and listened to Miss Glad as she read us a story. The only thing that was different in our kindergarten class, aside from the fact that we were handicapped, was that we had speech and physical therapy sessions.

A few months passed and I found myself with a book in my hands. Quite engrossed by it, I opened the book with uncontrollable movements.

"That word is *the*," I said out loud in my garbled speech pattern. "That word is *boy*."

Miss Glad, who was seated at her teacher's desk, suddenly looked at me and listened intensely. She became curious—very uncertain as to whether I was pretending to read or actually reading. She hesitated a bit longer before she approached me.

"Sweetie, which word is *the?*" Miss Glad asked as she took the book away from me and held it in a position so both of us could see.

Immediately, I pointed shakily to the word *the.*

She was surprised and asked, "Which word is *boy?*"

With a smile on my face, I pointed awkwardly to the word *boy.*

"Where did you learn to read, Sunshine?" she asked, as she gave me a gentle caress.

I just shrugged. It was much easier than to tell Miss Glad how I had learned to read. It was too hard for people to understand me.

But in my mind, I visualized Ms. Moody. Each day, at the Detroit Orthopedic Clinic, she would read a story out loud to the children. As we were mere babes (adorable enough to cuddle), Ms. Moody would love to sit a child upon her lap as she read to the other children who would be seated around her. Each child would be given a turn. On the times when I sat on Ms. Moody's lap, I remember that she would point to every word as she read it from the book. I was very observant.

Yeah, I must admit, that at first the letters on a page looked like nothing more than a big blur to me. But little by little, I began to pick up words. It was all absorbing, though. Not a soul knew that I could read, for I was a very shy little girl who never talked.

"Do you know any more words?" Miss Glad asked.

Sadly, I shook my head no. Upon my gesture, Miss Glad nurtured my inclinations to read that morning and mornings after that. I grew to love this fine teacher. She taught me to read with such patient teaching skills.

My progress in Miss Glad's special educational class-room was rapid. Perhaps my progress in reading was a reflection of my affliction. My relatively sedentary kind of existence led me toward introversion and early inclination toward sedentary activities with books rather than handicraft activities. I could not easily have derived satisfaction from activities involving my hands because I could not and cannot control them. I could not run or play as do normal children.

Also, I couldn't communicate well through speech. Vocal communication was difficult. But I could see well, and I was mentally sound in every aspect. The one activity from which I might derive maximum satisfaction was reading. I learned to read with much enthusiasm.

By the middle of the school year, without my knowledge Miss Glad did two wonderful things. First, she personally confided my great progress to my mother in a telephone call to my home. She invited my mother to visit our classroom and to see a demonstration of my reading skills. Second, she arranged with Miss Sung, another special education teacher, for my immediate transfer to Miss Sung's classroom and my promotion to regular grade status at the first-grade level.

On that occasion, as I was seated next to Miss Glad at a table, she opened a reading book and held it in a position so that both of us could see. Before us stood my mother and Miss Sung. Around us, the other children played merrily with puzzles and games.

"Loreena, read to your mother and Miss Sung."

Shyly, I looked at Miss Glad and hesitated.

"Pretend that your mother and Miss Sung aren't watching."

With that encouragement I started reading in an unnatural voice. " 'Dick and Jane have a dog named Spot.' "

Out of the corner of my eye, I noticed Miss Sung and my mother walking toward us. They stopped behind me and watched for themselves the sentences that I was reading from the book.

"Good, go on to the next page," Miss Glad cheered.

" 'Spot ran after the big red ball!' "

"Oh, my God," Mother cried, "she is really reading. My baby is reading." Mother stooped down and gave me a big hug and a kiss.

Miss Glad smiled and said, "I think we should tell her now!"

Puzzled, I looked at my teacher.

"Sweetheart, kindergarten isn't for you anymore. You are going into the first grade. Miss Sung here is going to be your new teacher," Miss Glad informed me, as she closed the reading book and laid it on the table.

Feeling as thrilled as a naive young college graduate who has just received special honors, I embraced my teacher and garbled, "Wow, first grade. Me!" My mother and Miss Glad broke out laughing.

"Would you like to come to see my classroom now, Sunshine?" Miss Sung asked as she stooped down to my level. Agreeing eagerly, I nodded. Then Miss Sung untied me from the chair and lifted me into her arms.

Sad good-byes passed between Miss Glad and me that day, I do recall. Oh, how hard it was to say good-bye to the first teacher who set me on the track toward my education. Many tears fell from my eyes as Miss Sung carried me out of the classroom.

Seconds later, still in the arms of Miss Sung and accompanied by my mother, I found myself in Miss Sung's special education classroom.

For those of you who don't know what a special education or "orthopedic" classroom is, please let me explain. A special education classroom is something like a schoolhouse used to be back in the early days—a large schoolroom with one teacher instructing students from kindergarten through twelfth grade, the only difference being that we were all physically or mentally challenged in some way.

Miss Sung hospitably demonstrated for us how she worked with her class and introduced me to her students. She explained that she taught grade levels one through six, and right then I knew that she was another fine teacher.

Once again, in my first-grade studies, I progressed quite rapidly. Immediately, Miss Sung set me to work with the other first graders, and I adjusted and participated well in my group. I felt quite comfortable in my new class and couldn't wait to learn, for I thirsted for knowledge. However, there was one major problem—the inability to write, due to a nerve overflow in my arms, which made the task of writing insurmountable!

It wasn't until a few months later that Miss Sung grew deeply concerned with over my inability to write. She had to be my writer and willingly wrote for me the schoolwork she prepared as I dictated my answers to her. Only by this means was written communication possible for me. She knew that a better solution to the problem was necessary if I were to successfully pursue my ambitions for an education. She explored the problem thoroughly and finally decided that the use of an electric typewriter was the answer to this problem! She spoke directly to the principal of Chippendale School, Mr. Mark, about the idea. He was willing to give his full cooperation and submitted a requisition for a typewriter.

One morning, Mr. Pitts had just carried me into the school building and stood me by my walker when I heard Miss Sung's voice: "Hurry up, Sunshine. It's here!"

A feeling of excitement gripped me. Smiling from ear to ear, I grabbed my walker and tried to hurry down to my classroom, wobbling to and fro as if I had had one too many drinks. No matter how much I tried to hurry, it was useless.

I wore heavy metal braces on my legs, which made the task of walking even more difficult. At that point of my life, Miss McDoe, the physical therapist at Chippendale School, gave Mr. Pitts firm orders not to carry me down to class anymore. She wanted me to be self-reliant as much as possible.

"It's about time, Sunshine," Miss Sung said, as she greeted me at the classroom door and assisted me off with my coat. "Head your little self over to the typewriter, while I go hang up your coat. Please, do it quietly. Do not disturb the others."

Eagerly, I nodded.

Miss Sung adminstered to her student body, composed of handicapped children of varying ages and grade levels, with methodical grouping, compassionate discipline, careful timing, and skilled and devoted teaching. She was able, as only a skilled and dedicated teacher can be, to teach us fundamental academic subjects.

She managed to elicit the best response from all of us, from her mentally retarded group, to whom she taught simple word associations and handicrafts, to her more advanced sixth-grade group. We all loved her, respected her, and depended upon her. We needed her guidance, trustingly wanted her to lead us, and sought her approval and recognition. Oh, how we admired her.

Within minutes, I stood transfixed beside the typewriter, with my mouth opened wide, and my eyes riveted to the odd-looking machine. It wasn't a plain ordinary typewriter. It had special features on it. Over the green keys sat a special keyboard and in the back of it was a roll of paper attached to the black machine.

"Strange looking, isn't it?" Miss Sung whispered.

I nodded and asked in an unnatural voice, "Miss Sung, what is the roll of paper doing there?"

"Boy, you are a smart cookie. What else does it have that an ordinary typewriter doesn't?"

Immediately, I pointed waveringly to the special keyboard.

"Can't pull the wool over your eyes, can I?"

I shook my head, smiling.

It was then that she explained that the special keyboard resting over the keys was there so I could not strike more than one key at a time. The roll of paper attached to the back of the typewriter was there so that I didn't have to put paper into it—which I couldn't do since I can't control my arm movements.

Miss Sung began to show me how to communicate using this wonderful gift—the typewriter. Today, typewriters are almost extinct and out-of-date. The "in" thing of our modern society is that marvelous invention—computers. Each house has one! But back in the late fifties and early sixties, the typewriter was the "in" thing, and I was very privileged to have been given one. Miss Sung continued the instructions until I was able to use the typewriter alone. At first I was awkward at it, like a new tot learning to walk, not knowing what finger to use to press down on a key. Then I began to use my right thumb, pressing down a key quite slowly (ninety seconds a letter). Gradually the remedy to my inability to write became a functional reality. The typewriter was the instrument that paved the way for my rapid and successful progress in spelling skills.

When I could manage the typewriter and was depending upon it regularly to complete my written schoolwork assignments, Miss McDoe, my physical therapist, recommended to Miss Sung that I be supported by a rigid doorlike board at my back, and I was surrounded on the other three sides as well. Facing me was the table top. This box-like cubicle is called a standing table. From a standing position, I would do all of my typing, thereby exercising my leg muscles as well as fingers, hand, and arm ligaments and muscles. This became newsworthy to the extent that a reporter of a local newspaper visited our school and wrote the following story:

The caption under the photo read: "A Child Learns to Communicate." His story described how a young cerebral palsy victim, unable to talk, was being taught to communicate through an electric typewriter by two of the center's orthopedic instructors, Ruth Sung and Marsha Glad. "Because of the severity of her affliction, the little girl is supported in a box-like cubicle, which enables her to operate the machine."

I consider his journalism a bit insensitive. It might have been more appropriate to state, " . . . with a severe speech impediment . . . ," instead of, "unable to talk. . . . " Really, undue credit might have been given to Miss Glad in the newspaper account, which erroneously omitted mention of Miss McDoe, the therapist who'd proposed the standing table for me.

It is entirely unknown to me if Miss Glad recommended typewriting lessons to Miss Sung, who actually taught me to type. In any case, I am most grateful for the publicity, particularly because it made known an innovation in education that I am sure has aided other handicapped children.

On the last day of school, Miss Sung distributed report cards to all of her students. I had never had a report card before, so I had Miss Sung open it for me. Tears of joy streamed down my cheeks when I noticed that I had received all As and a note to my parents that read, "Your daughter is one of my brightest students! She is always willing to learn with such eagerness. She will definitely be in second grade next fall, and I am planning on sending her off to a reading class with nonhandicapped children. Have a great summer, and please take good care of my Sunshine."

My second-grade school year at Chippendale started much too soon. Like all summer vacations, that summer flew by. Yet I didn't seem to mind, for I loved school, and I loved Miss Sung.

On my first day back, Miss Sung took me down to the reading class and left me there with Mrs. Hart, who was the second-grade reading teacher for the nonhandicapped students. Even at that age of my life, I knew that I had a speech problem, and I knew that I would face cruel remarks from the children when I did speak. I was quite surprised when not one child made a cruel remark that day or on the days that followed when I attempted to articulate as I read out loud to the class. From that first session, I was made to feel welcome as a member of the group.

Oh, how I do recall the feeling I had on that very first day in Mrs. Hart's class. It seemed as if a million butterflies fluttered around in my stomach as I sat at a large, round table with able-bodied boys and girls. I swallowed hard and shyly focused my eyes down on the reading book that was held open by Mrs. Hart, who sat next to me.

"This is Loreena, boys and girls," Mrs. Hart introduced me, and added, "She is coming to our reading class every day from now on. Loreena, would you like to begin our story for today?"

Once again, I swallowed hard. I hesitated for a bit, and then, unclearly, read out loud, " 'One day, Dick and Jane walked across the street.' "

Mrs. Hart interpreted my words so the class could understand what I'd said. The boys and girls all looked at one another, for they never heard anyone with a speech problem before. Surprisingly, they did not giggle.

"Donald, will you read the next sentence?" Mrs. Hart asked the little boy.

The little boy smiled as he read the next sentence out

loud. Each child read a sentence until the entire story was read, during which time Mrs. Hart asked us questions about the story.

By the end of that first week, I felt a warm acceptance. I was becoming less of an oddity and more of a familiar face.

Miss Sung taught her students just like the year before, grouping us by our grade levels and working with each group daily. Each group would gather around a circular table and she would teach us spelling, math, reading, history, and science, as well as other subjects.

While she worked with each group, the rest of us would be sitting quietly at our desks, working on our assignments. This class had no radio or television to divert our attention from our studies. There were recess times. Yet there was a professional atmosphere that we all needed and cherished.

"Boys and girls, please close your books and look up here," Miss Sung said one day, as she stood in front of the big blackboard. We all obeyed.

"Now, boys and girls, whose birthday is it today?"

In unison we all yelled, "George Washington's."

"Correct. Who was he? Please, raise your hand and don't shout out the answer."

A few children raised their hands, but Miss Sung called upon a fourth grader, who yelled, "Our first president of the United States!"

"Loreena," Miss Sung called. "What is today's date?"

"February 22nd," I answered.

"And what year was he born in, David?"

"Seventeen hundred and thirty-two," David, a sixth grader, shouted.

Miss Sung then smiled as she walked over to the door and, in a half-broken voice, shouted "You may come in now, George Washington!"

Our chins dropped, and with bewildered faces, we sat

completely motionless, except for one little girl, a first grader, who cheered, "Our president is here to see us!"

"You nitwit, he died on December 14, 1799!" David, the sixth grader, shouted back to the little girl.

Who is outside of our classroom door? we all wondered. *Could it be that he came back to life?* Our puzzled looks turned to laughter as soon as Miss Sung opened the door and in walked a little, white fuzzy lamb. Our roaring laughter frightened the poor little lamb, causing him to stop dead in his tracks. He looked at us as if to say, "Why are you all laughing at me?"

"Quiet down, boys and girls," Miss Sung ordered. "There are other classes in session. Can anyone tell me why they think the lamb is named after our first president, George Washington?"

Immediately, I raised my hand.

"Yes, Sunshine," Miss Sung called as she walked back to the blackboard.

"Could it be that he was born on Washington's birthday?" I blurted out.

"That's correct!"

Miss Sung asked us many more questions about the first president of the United States.

The real event started when "George" decided to leave droppings on the floor. Craig Nesbett, a boy who walked with crutches, and a boy on whom I had a terrible crush, trailed the small lamb around with a broom and dustpan in hand, cleaning up George's mess. I still remember Craig's face each time George left his droppings. He made such funny faces, everyone broke into hysterical laughter.

I can't speak for the others, but I laughed so hard that day that my stomach was sore for a whole week. Wow, what fun was had by all! We also fed George milk from a baby bottle and petted the little creature. That was a George Washington's birthday that will always remain with me.

Days flew into months, and soon my second-grade school year ended. On the last day of school, it was both a time of much joy and of much sadness. I remember Miss Sung motioned for me to come up to her desk. I grabbed my walker and went to her.

"Do you want to sit on my lap or in a chair, Sunshine?" I quickly pointed to her lap, and she lifted me up.

"My, my, still so tiny. I bet your leg braces weigh more than you. Don't you suppose so?"

I let out a few giggles as I shrugged. I watched as she reached and snatched up a brown envelope from her desk.

"What's that?" I asked.

"Guess?"

"Is it my report card?"

She nodded and pulled it out from the envelope. "You did quite well in Mrs. Hart's reading class. How did you enjoy her class?"

I beamed with delight and said, "I loved it! I thought that the kids were going to laugh at me when I read out loud, but no, they didn't!"

"How nice. Mrs. Hart gave you an A. See?" Miss Sung said, as she positioned the report card in front of me.

For a few seconds, I just sat there, completely engrossed by the grade markings that I was reading silently to myself. Once again, I'd received all As, with a note stating, "Dear Mr. and Mrs. Minaudo, your daughter has completed second grade and will be going into the third grade this fall. It has been a joy teaching her. I've never seen a child so thirsty for knowledge as Loreena is. I feel very comforted that Loreena's school years will be bright due to the use of the typewriter. Please take care of my Sunshine. I won't be back in the fall, Love, Miss Ruth Sung."

I broke into tears. The last sentence broke my heart into tiny pieces. I turned and threw my arms around her neck, and through my sobs, I said, "Please, don't go, Miss Sung."

She held me tight and swallowed hard. I don't think she had expected such a reaction from me. I hated good-byes when I loved someone, and I loved this fine woman.

"We must leave, my little one."

" 'We?' " I questioned.

"Miss Glad and Miss McDoe are leaving too."

My sobs deepened as I thought, *How can they leave us!*

"Loreena, settle down before I cry too. We did our jobs here, and now it's time to move on. Other children need us now," Miss Sung said, as she reached for a Kleenex and dried off my tears.

"I love you, Miss Sung. We need you to stay here," I begged.

Miss Sung consoled me for a few minutes longer, and then she stood me back at my walker. I kissed her and saw tears fall from her eyes. She quickly wiped them away. With her permission, I went to say my good-byes to Miss Glad and Miss McDoe. Oh, such a sad day it was! It was like a rainy day. Tears kept falling. I was, I felt, losing three wonderful friends.

You see, when you are handicapped, you feel as if you are living inside of a balloon. Not many people want to talk or get close to you, especially when you have a speech impairment. Yet these three special angels were always willing to listen and spend time with me and the others.

I knew then that I was most grateful to Miss Glad for teaching me how to read; Miss Sung for teaching me how to communicate through the use of an electric typewriter; and Miss McDoe, the fine and tireless therapist, for seeking with all the skill she had to improve not just one part of my body

34

but every part, including my hands, legs, speech, and facial muscles.

I cried all the way home that day. Each of these fine teachers had brought something into my life and imprinted it in some way that has remained with me throughout my school years and throughout the rest of my life.

When I look back upon all of my wonderful and devoted schoolteachers at Chippendale, Miss Sung's name always comes to my mind. I guess it's because she provided my limited world with light by teaching me how to type. She paved my way and opened my mind to knowledge.

The most incredible thing about Miss Sung is that she was ahead of her time. By this I mean that mainstreaming, also known as inclusion, was hardly ever practiced in the early 1960s. Yet this marvelous woman sent me off to a regular reading class when I was in second grade. She believed, as I feel strongly now, that all physically challenged children should go to school with able-bodied children. It has occurred to me more than once that if Miss Sung had stayed at Chippendale for another year, I might have been completely inclusioned. I believe so. But fate wasn't kind, and I grieve this loss.

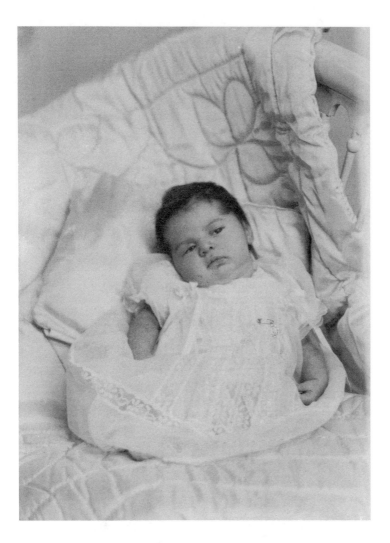

Loreena's christening day at one month.

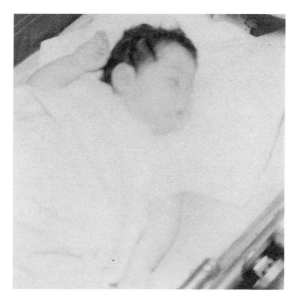

Loreena napping at four months.

Loreena at eight months with her mom.

Loreena at nine months having fun in the sun with her kiddy car.

Loreena with her brother, Peter, rubbing her eye at two years.

Loreena with her dad under an orange tree in Florida at three years.

Brother Peter with his sister, enjoying the Florida weather.

Loreena in her first car at age four.

Loreena loves to swing on her swing.

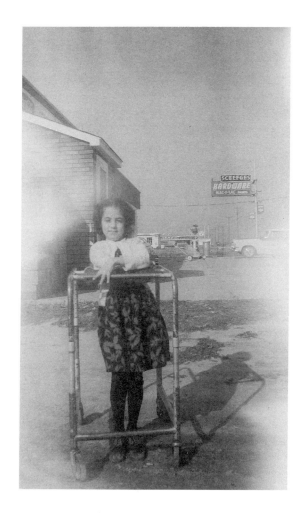

Loreena in her walker.

Loreena at her high school graduation.

Loreena at the Macomb Community College grounds.

Chapter Three
More Chippendale Years

Such fine memories I have of my third-grade year at Chippendale. I remember that I was filled with much excitement, and I couldn't wait to know who our new teacher would be. I was awkwardly trying to hurry to my classroom with my walker, when suddenly a classmate came running up to me.

"Loreena, guess what? We have a man for a teacher. He's cute, too!" Judy informed me.

I giggled. "Really?"

She nodded, turned, and skipped back to the classroom. Judy Smith was a lovely little girl with dark brown hair and eyes. That day she wore a pretty mint green–colored skirt with a white blouse. We were both third graders, and really, she was the first friend I had in school.

I was told that when Judy was an infant she had had a very high fever, which resulted in a very slight speech impairment and a slight limp when she walked. But there were many times when I would wonder why she was in an orthopedic class, for to me, she wasn't as unfortunate as the rest of us were.

I entered the classroom shyly, yet smiling from ear to ear.

"Hello, sweetheart! I'm Mr. Burke. What's your name?"

"Loreena."

"Pardon me?"

"Loreena," I garbled again.

"I'm sorry, can you say it again?" He was having a difficult time understanding me.

"Loreena," I garbled again as clearly as I could.

"Loreena! Aren't you the little girl Miss Sung taught to communicate through the use of an electric typewriter?"

I nodded yes.

"Here, let me help you off with your sweater before Mr. Mark comes," Mr. Burke said, referring to our principal. He started unbuttoning my sweater for me and took it off.

"Thanks," I said with a smile.

Mr. Burke winked, and he motioned for me to go sit with the others at the large table. I nodded and went over to take a seat next to Judy.

"Told ya he is cute," Judy whispered into my ear. I smiled, beaming with much joy. How wonderful it felt being back in school.

Mr. Burke led us in the Pledge of Allegiance, and we recited after him as best we could. According to the type of disability we had, some children stood while others sat in wheelchairs with their right hands placed over their hearts as they recited. Mr. Mark walked into our classroom and quietly headed over to us. He stood in silence until we were through with the Pledge of Allegiance.

"Boys and girls, may I have your attention?" Mr. Mark said as soon as we were through.

Judy and I looked at one another. We were both baffled.

"Boys and girls, we have a new physical therapist. Her name is Miss Mall. And we have a new kindergarten teacher. However, Mr. Burke will be your substitute teacher for a while. We are unable to find a permanent teacher for your class," Mr. Mark said. Then he looked at Mr. Burke, adding, "These children are here to be educated. We're not here to pity them. Yes, it's sad that they have the misfortune of being disabled, but we must enrich their lives by education."

Mr. Mark paused for a moment and then explained to Mr. Burke each of our names, the type of affliction we had, and the grade we were about to enter. He then walked over to the bookcase, opened it, and started to pass out schoolbooks.

Thus the year began. I still stood at the standing table, with locked braces, typing all of my assignments on the electric typewriter quite slowly with my right thumb. Due to the extreme movements of my arms, it took me about ninety seconds to hit just one key on the keyboard, so you can imagine how long it took to complete an assignment! That year I ran into a problem. Like all third graders, I had begun to learn multiplication tables and fractions. The typewriter did not have keys with fractions, and I didn't know what to do. With a struggle, I raised my hand, and Mr. Burke came over to see what was wrong.

"Mr. Burke, I am having trouble. I don't know how to do these fractions on the typewriter. What am I to do?" I cried, pointing with unstable movements of the fractions in my arithmetic book.

"Hon, can't you write at all?"

I sadly shook my head no, acutely feeling my handicap. Mr. Burke looked down at the keyboard, not saying a word for a long time. Suddenly, he smiled and said, "I've got it, kid! In order to type a fraction, you must push three keys down. The numerator, then the slash key, and then the denominator. Like this."

He then typed, "1/2, 8/9."

My eyes widened as I watched him demonstrate on the typewriter. "Wow, that's neat!" I mumbled. And the problem was solved, thanks to Mr. Burke.

One day there was a bit of entertainment being presented in the school gym for the pleasure of the children. This time the entertainment lasted an hour or so, featuring animated cartoons. A thought suddenly took hold of me. I did not want to sit still for that long a time and endure what the others considered enjoyable. I made believe I was ill. I bent over and acted as though I were about to puke. A classmate sitting next to me noticed and called Mrs. Clark. She was the helper-aide who cared for us. Such an incident usually receives prompt attention in a school where there are handicapped children.

Mrs. Clark walked over to me and said softly, "What's wrong, Loreena. Don't you feel well?"

"No, I feel sick to my stomach," I replied weakly. I really did hate to watch cartoons.

Immediately, Mrs. Clark grabbed a wheelchair, sat me in it, and quickly wheeled me to the teachers' lounge, where Mr. Burke sat, having a cup of coffee.

"We have a sick little girl here, Mr. Burke," Mrs. Clark said, as we entered the lounge.

Mr. Burke put down his cup of coffee and walked over to me. Mrs. Clark left the room. Mr. Burke felt my forehead to see if I was feverish.

I was not a very good liar, and when he said, "You look all right to me," I felt guilty and decided to confess what I had done. The guilt was a bit much to bear and tears began to roll down my cheeks. When Mr. Burke saw what was happening, he wheeled me over to a large table and sat in a nearby chair for the conversation he sensed was imminent. By now the tears were gushing down my face, but he was kind and patient.

So, between sobs, I tried to explain my dislike for cartoons. He listened, and he understood. He was disturbed, though, by my incessant sobbing. I had never lied before and the guilty feeling lay heavily on my heart so that my tears and sobs were now becoming uncontrollable. That prevented him from either counseling or comforting me. Finally, his calming words and attitude soothed me so that I regained some control and could listen.

He said, "That's not the Loreena I know. The Loreena I know always has a smile on her face."

I began to feel better.

He next asked, "Did you lie because you hate to watch cartoon movies?"

With an apologetic look on my face, I timidly nodded my head affirmatively. He laughed a little, and he succeeded in making me laugh at myself by telling me about a school prank of his that he had been too afraid to confide to either his parents or his teacher.

Mr. Burke and I parted best of friends that day, each of us vowing never to tell our secrets to anyone. They were only to be kept between the two of us. My feelings toward Mr. Burke will forever be warm, though I knew him for only a little while. About two weeks later, he was transferred elsewhere.

We had another substitute, and another.

Each taught us extremely well, though, thanks to Mr. Mark, who preached to each substitute, as he had that very first day to Mr. Burke, how vitally important it was for us to receive a good education. I believe he instructed our class to be run as Miss Sung wanted it, for it was run the same way. Each day each grade level would sit around the table for about an hour or so learning English, arithmetic, history, spelling, and science. Then we were given our assignments to do on our own, while each of the other grades took their turn in a session at the table for instructions.

Yet after about seven months, we just hated working with new teachers every fifteen days or so. One day a new substitute overheard us as we moaned, "Oh, no, not another substitute!" Her name has escaped me, but little did we know that this fine lady would not be just another sub. She apparently accepted what she overheard that day as a challenge, for she immediately set about the business of teaching us as much as she could of academic learning with an earnest and constant effort and a full heart.

She reviewed and retaught—by way of our textbooks, papers, and worksheets—subject matter that each of us had failed to grasp or in which we needed strengthening, and covered with each of us new subject matter. She came to know each of us well very quickly and worked hard with all of us throughout her six-week stay.

One day, Mr. Mark made another announcement. He told us that our fine teacher had appealed to the Board of Education to amend and adjust a rule that stipulated that substitute teachers could not serve in one given teaching assignment for more than fifteen school days, so that such teachers might be permitted to serve in one position as long as they were needed. Second, he told us that our teacher had made this appeal so that she could remain with our class until the end of the school year. Third, he said that he had good news. Her appeal had been granted by the Board of Education. With the greatest of enthusiasm, we all applauded Mr. Mark's announcement. I am sure our teacher felt the greatest of pride at our applause. She walked through the aisles between our seats and patted each of us, as she bent down so we could kiss her on the cheek.

I'll never forget the last day of that school year, not just because I was granted promotion from third to fourth grade, which in itself is memorable. Although no special occasion was planned and none ever discussed, each child who came to school that last morning—just as if one child read another's mind—had a gift especially wrapped for our teacher, which we handled with tender care and gave to her with a smile that indicated our heartfelt gratitude.

I saw tears well up in her eyes several times that day, especially when she received the gifts; when she spoke to us near the end of the day, thanking us for our kind gifts and telling us that she was happy to have been our teacher; and finally, when she kissed each of us on the cheek and wished us a happy summer vacation.

Judy Smith and I became the best of friends. I have a lot of fond memories of her, but the fondest of them all was the time, during our fourth-grade school year, when we were invited down to the gym to see a bit of entertainment. Once again, Judy and I sat next to each other. The year was 1963—the time when the Beatles had just arrived from London and all of America had gone wild.

The lights in the gym were dimmed, as we sat among two hundred able-bodied children who were seated cross-legged on the floor, anticipating the performance to start. I remember the children's whispers and soft laughter spreading like wild fires around the room. I also remember hearing the "hushes" from teachers who tried to quiet their recalcitrant students.

Suddenly, the blue velvet curtain opened, and the laughter and whispers stopped. On the lighted stage before us stood four little boys. Three of the boys had toy guitars and the other had drums. These boys all had on wigs, and it was very obvious that they were imitating the Beatles. In the background, a record by the Beatles, "I Want to Hold Your Hand," was playing. We sat still, in awe, listening and watching the performers.

Then, suddenly, after they'd lip-synched four or five Beatle tunes, Judy tapped me on my shoulder and said, "Let's do it."

"Do what?" I whispered.

"Scream like teenagers do on television."

I hesitated.

"C'mon, chicken," Judy said as she let out a few cackling sounds.

"Cut it out. I'll do it, but you go first."

She smiled, and let out a forceful scream. Then I did. Soon our screams spread throughout the audience. Everyone got into the act. Miss Tom, our teacher, and Mrs. Clark sought us out of the crowd, put us over their knees, and paddled our behinds in tune to the music. Little did they know that they stole the show. It caused the crowd of children to go wild.

We thought we would never stop laughing; our teachers who were, of course, only acting could not contain themselves and burst out laughing, too. The principal came in to quiet the turmoil and could not hold back his laughter. So a grand time was had by all. It must have been a full twenty minutes or so before the entire roomful of us regained composure and recovered from the chaos instigated by Judy and me. With such uncontrollable laughter, it was hard to remember that this was a school day.

About two months later, I was told that my best friend had died from pneumonia. Back then I just didn't understand how very sick the poor little girl was. All I knew was that she bore no visible signs of being a severely handicapped child. Yet Judy was subject to epileptic seizures and convulsions, which occurred more and more frequently and became less and less controllable with each passing day of her life.

I remember that the shock of Judy's death gripped me so much that I just sat there for days motionless, with my heart filled with pain. One afternoon, my mother came to me and sat next to me on our couch. In comfort, she put her arms around me, opened her little black leather Bible, and started reading out loud this passage from Ecclesiastes 3:

" 'There is an appointed time for everything, and a time for every affair under the heavens. A time to be born, and a time to die; a time to plant, and a time to uproot the plant; a time to kill, and a time to heal; a time to tear down, and a time to build. A time to weep, and a time to laugh; a time to mourn, and a time to dance. A time to scatter stones, and a time to gather them; a time to embrace, and a time to be far from embraces. A time to seek, and a time to lose; a time to keep, and a time to cast away. A time to rend, and a time to sew; a time to be silent, and a time to speak. A time to love, and a time to hate; a time of war, and a time of peace.' "

The Bible verse that Mother read did not soothe me then, or even for days following. Judy's death hit me much too hard—so hard that I couldn't hold any food in when I ate. I would feel sick to my stomach, very sick.

Like any concerned parent, Mother took me to the family doctor, and he prescribed medication for an upset stomach—more strong than Pepto-Bismol, which did help, but it took me about a month to recuperate from my friend's death—after many hours of sitting silently, asking God, *Why? Why did He take my best friend away from me?*

In that year, Miss Tom increased my knowledge of geography by drawing blank maps of the seven continents and making me fill in the blanks. These were all done on the typewriter, and I found geography exciting and fun! However, when it came to history, I found it to be boring and dull. History was just not my cup of tea, and it still isn't! Yet due to Miss Tom's teachings, I learned quite well.

My favorite subject, though, was arithmetic. Due to my irregular arm movements, I couldn't jot anything down, so I learned to add, divide, subtract, and multiply all in my head, and then type just the answer down. My answers would always be correct, and I owe this ability to my dad. He was a genius when it came to math. We both found it easy and did it with a snap of a finger.

During that year, a trip to a macaroni factory was planned and implemented by Miss Tom. A chartered bus, especially assigned for the trip, picked us up. Three of the school personnel, Miss Tom, Miss Mall and Mrs. Clark, assisted and attended us. Their tasks were not easy ones, and their responsibilties were indeed great. While an excursion of this kind, merely an outing of a few hours, is usually a simple routine for an ordinary classroom of children my age, such a trip becomes a major undertaking—a very serious project—for a class of severely handicapped children.

We each needed to be helped individually—virtually every step of the way. We needed assistance getting onto the bus, into our seats, out of our seats, and off the bus. Some children were carried, some were wheeled, and some slowly were escorted on foot. The teachers who accompanied us had their hands full, even though each of the children was willing and eager to help the other. The more mobile children enthusiastically and unselfishly tried to help those less mobile. To every child the anticipation of the long bus ride and a new experience filled with new things to see meant that a grand time was in store for us.

Along with the joy and excitement of the occasion, the spirit of love and laughter was very evident. Happiness was obvious on every child's face, and endless sounds of it rang out among all the children. The scene paralleled the scene of a joyous group of children leaving on an extensive vacation trip, yet ours was to last just a little while.

Voices were heard everywhere, shouting such things as "When are we leaving?" and "I can't hardly wait to get there."

Because of the detailed care required to transport severely handicapped children, the time-consuming preparation, and the safety risks, trips away from school were, generally speaking, less frequent for us than for regular children. So when we had such a treat, or in fact any special treat, we were thrilled to the limit.

There were only sixteen of us, but we were, in all candor, a handful, albeit a happy "handful." Since a trip like the one we were taking involves no small amount of walking, wheelchairs were loaded on our bus so that any child whose endurance would not permit him or her to do all the walking could ride at least part of the time.

We shouted for joy as the bus pulled away from the curb. The seats closest to the windows were, of course, the most coveted ones but we were given no choice, and those not so fortunate as to sit near a window contented themselves with a more distant view of the passing scene. We were all so happy to be going, even the few chronic complainers among my classmates. The driver calmly and skillfully guided his huge vehicle through miles of traffic, unperturbed by our happy, continuous jabbering, and in about twenty minutes, we arrived at our destination. Considering the ride and our natural and customary impatience, I must say that on that occasion we were, on the whole, well behaved. The teachers who accompanied us expressed their gratitude and their wish for an equally pleasant return trip.

When each of us had been assisted individually from our seats on the bus and then escorted off the bus, and when those who needed to use wheelchairs were finally settled in them, it was realized that there were more occupied wheelchairs than there were people to push them. So the three teachers who accompanied us each tried to handle two wheelchairs. They worked hard, and they managed.

Finally, we entered the main door of the building housing the macaroni factory where our guide, a pleasant-appearing, energetic gent greeted us. He was most cordial, and he seemed very enthusiastic as he said in a soft but very audible and well-articulated voice, "Hello, boys and girls." Whereupon, in unison, we dutifully returned the same greeting in what unintentionally sounded like raucous thunder. He continued to speak, saying simply, "I will show you around and explain to all of you each point of interest on our tour."

As he led the way, we gazed wide-eyed upon huge vats

of copper and galvanized metal and huge pieces of stainless steel equipment. We were immediately impressed with the immaculate cleanliness of the entire premises and its contents. All the equipment looked scrubbed, shiny, and absolutely dustless. I, for one, marveled at the spotlessness; it never occurred to me that a factory could be that clean. Our guide paused now and then in front of a huge piece of equipment and he explained interestingly and clearly, unfolding the process so that we all could understand just how, from beginning to end, macaroni is prepared and packaged for use by the homemaker or the restauranteur.

We were amazed to see such massive quantities of pasta being prepared by machines that could do so much work by merely the flick of a switch. So deft, exact, and versatile were the machines that we actually saw relatively fewer workers than we expected engaged in this kind of factory work. One or two attendants could operate a huge machine, or supervise its operation, by means of switches that set whole processes in motion and continued to completion. When it ended, a single attendant reloaded a machine and began the process anew.

I thought of my mother, who was always known to be a capable and efficient cook, who could, and still can, prepare homemade pasta for her family in an hour and a half from simple ingredients by preparing the dough, drying it, and then cutting it. Yet in a matter of minutes, these marvelous machines, with little supervision, did all this effortlessly in a quantity sufficient to feed a whole population of people.

It was amazing to see the packaging process whereby, in minutes, hundreds of packages of the product were readied for markets. We were indeed witnessing our first glimpse of mass production. About ten women dressed in clean white smocks and seated at a large, elongated table formed a packaging assembly line. By using prepared cardboard packages, already labeled and filled with a set amount of spaghetti, they completed the packaging process by sealing the cartons.

When our guide completed the tour of the plant with us, he escorted us back to the main entrance, where we each gladly accepted a bottle of soda pop. Our tour of the plant assured us that the product we were buying in supermarkets was a very clean and wholesome one. We thanked the guide for an enjoyable and informative tour and left to board the bus, climbing into our seats and reloading our wheelchairs.

When the bus was again in motion, Miss Tom conducted class by discussing with us what our tour of the macaroni factory should have taught us. She asked questions and called upon us to answer. This question-and-answer discussion sharpened and clarified our tour observations. This indeed had been, I thought, a school day well spent.

Once again, I received good grades and passed into the fifth grade. That year our teacher was Mrs. Hold, who taught us extremely well. I will always remember her standing in front of the standing table each Friday morning, reading off a list of words from her spelling text, words on which I was tested. Mrs. Hold exhibited patience every time she read a word, for she would then wait until I would type it. Very slowly, but surely, I would type letter by letter until I would spell a word out. Each Friday my spelling test would consist of twenty words, and out of them I would get one or two wrong.

In lower grades in school, all of my schoolbooks were softcovered, filled with pages in which I, or any other child, could write the answers. I remember that I was a little fuss-budget when it came to my books. I would type down my answers on a sheet of paper and have the teacher or my mother fill in the blanks in my book. One day, Mr. Mark became our substitute for Mrs. Hold, who became ill. I guess I asked him to fill in my worksheet for me, for the next thing

I knew he abruptly started tearing the sheet from my workbook and placing it in the typewriter.

He instructed me to do the lesson on the sheet. Unaccustomed to the brusque attitude that Mr. Mark demonstrated on that occasion, I worked through tears. I, however, accomplished all of the work and double-checked it. When I later, shyly, gave him my work, he smilingly and questioningly looked down at me as if he were asking, "Well, did you get the message?" Then he eagerly scanned my worksheet, and his smile broadened with a look of pleasure.

I did get the message. I began to realize that I was imposing upon my teacher and my mother for help more than necessary. After that, I accomplished more of my work alone. It was sometimes done less perfectly, but it was my own work. I corrected my errors myself, learned much more, and pleased Mrs. Hold.

One day, Mrs. Hold asked, "Loreena, what are you doing?"

"Working on the arithmetic assignment that you gave me."

"Oh, no, you don't. It's recess time," Mrs. Hold said as she reached and turned off the switch from the electric typewriter and added, "It's a beautiful spring day out there!"

"Please don't make me take recess. I want to do my assignment," I begged.

I hated recess! Due to my handicap, especially my speech impairment, I would try to avoid playing with the children for fear they would make fun of me. Yet I was a lonely little girl, who wanted and needed friends.

"Nothing doing, Loreena. What am I going to do with you? Every recess it is like pulling teeth to get you to stop working," Mrs. Hold scolded as she took me out of the standing table.

"Please, I don't want to," I whined.

"Yes! Do you want me to tickle you for the whole fifteen-minute break?" she asked as she walked me over to my walker and waited patiently for me to grab it.

"No!" I yelled.

"Then get!"

Once outside, I just loved it. The playground was crowded with able-bodied children from other classrooms, and their laughter and chattering was quite noisy. I was scared though, and even now, I'm not really sure why.

Most children played on seesaws, monkey bars, swings, and slides, while others played cops 'n' robbers, tag, jump rope, or other games. Both Mrs. Hold and Mrs. Clark stood near and chaperoned us. They didn't want us to get hit with a ball, nor did they want anyone to run into us and knock us down.

Sometimes, Mrs. Clark would put me on the swing, which I loved. Since my hands are weak, I couldn't hold onto things. I remember that I had to put my arms around the chains, and that is how I held on tightly to the chains of the swing. Oh, how I do recall the feeling of freedom that I felt and the wind on my face each time I would swing. And how very well I do remember the same conversation between Mrs. Clark and me. The coversation always went something like this:

"Higher, Mrs. Clark, higher!" I was a little dare-demon, who hated being pushed slowly.

"My heart is already in my mouth! What do you want, for me to have a heart attack?" she would answer with a laugh.

"Please, push me higher," I would plead.

"Heaven help us both!" Mrs. Clark would laugh as she gave me a bigger push, and add, "Please, hold on tightly, Loreena!"

My giggling would increase with every push. However,

I couldn't stay on for more than ten minutes because the chains would leave imprints on my skin and it would hurt.

At other times, when Mrs. Clark and Mrs. Hold were busy with the other children, I would walk around the playground with my walker wobbling, watching children play. I guess one of the able-bodied little girls I knew when I was in Mrs. Hart's first-grade reading class needed someone to twirl rope, and she asked Mrs. Hold if I could try.

"Ask Loreena yourself," she said.

Back then I was very shy and didn't talk to many kids my own age for fear that they might laugh at me. So when the little girl asked me, I shook my head no.

"Please, I want to play jump rope with Mary, and I'd like you to twirl the rope. I know you can!"

And with that encouragement, I took the rope with sweeping movements of my right hand, while I held on tightly to my walker with my left hand. To my surprise, I twirled better than I thought, and I liked it. From then on, I was the rope twirler!!!

In my sixth and seventh grades at Chippendale, Miss McCall taught us in our special education classroom. She was brand new, so to speak, having just graduated from the university. It was her first teaching job and she sparked with enthusiasm, giving each of her students all of her heart and soul when it came to teaching.

At that stage of my life, I was the oldest pupil and the only one in my grade. So Miss McCall taught me one on one. I don't know why I remember this, but she was the first teacher who insisted that I go to the library to take out a book each month and then write a report on it. I remember reading *Little Women* and *The Miracle Worker*, to name two.

Each year, just as with all students, my workload increased, and I found it much too tiring to stand at the standing table to type my school lessons. With Miss Mall's permission, I then began typing from a sitting position, which was much more comfortable and not as tiring. It wasn't until then that I changed my typing habit. It just didn't seem right typing with my right thumb from a sitting position. After a time, filled with much frustration and trying to figure out which finger to use, I started to type with the fourth finger of my left hand. It is the finger I still use today.

It was at this time that I no longer found arithmetic problems a simple matter of figuring inside of my head and typing down my answers. The problem solutions were now worked out in so much more intricate detail. Problems like 7,4804 x 4,326 were mind-boggling! So Miss McCall would sit next to me in my class period and jot down the answers I gave her. It was a lot easier for me that way.

I didn't like being the oldest child in the class, but it brought many insights by allowing me to be an observer of other children's afflictions. I observed the disease named muscular dystrophy, which mainly hits boys. Through the windows of my soul, I have seen boys, such as Steve and John Hadsell, and others, who routinely came happily walking into school as if nothing were wrong with them, then, suddenly begin to experience instances of falling until eventually they'd end up in wheelchairs. I have seen these beautiful angels grow weaker and weaker until they died.

I have seen children with cerebral palsy who did improve miraculously over the years. I have also observed other afflictions, such as hydrocephalus (water on the brain), spina bifida, the deaf, the blind, etc. Yet, as with all youngsters who are handicapped, we viewed ourselves as just children!

I remember play periods after lunch. During the winter months, the children would play indoors. They were, like all children, loud, noisy, and full of the dickens! Forget puzzles or games!! They wanted to play real games, like tag, musical chairs, or cops 'n' robbers! Oh, what a joyous feeling I would have when I saw a young child walking on crutches being chased by a child in a wheelchair—all in slow motion.

"I'm going to get you!"

"No, you're not!"

"Yes, I am! I can move my crutches faster than you."

"Can not!"

"Can too!"

Screaming and yelling would continue until one would be caught by the other. This was only one of the many games that went on during lunch break. Unfortunately, due to my being a very slow eater, I would just have time for lunch and didn't have time to play.

I find nothing really negative to say about Chippendale School. However, I believe that the teachers could have improved our lives by showing us educational films illustrating the positive and negative aspects of life. For instance, they could have shown films on how to make friends, or what to say to a person who makes fun of your disability, or to think of yourself with a positive image!

Perchance, in the 1960s they didn't have films of this nature, which, if true, is very sad! I know these types of films would have enhanced my life. You see, I was, and I still am, filled with a lot of fears. One of my fears back then was the fear of being laughed at. This was the reason why I would avoid recess time. So I would hide within myself! Now that I look back on it, I was just plain foolish! Not all able-bodied children are cruel. So you may find one bad apple in a bushel, but so what? Life has many hills. Some you may climb and reach the top; on others you may slip and fall. But that's life.

Another fear at that time was coping with death. You see, Judy Smith wasn't the only schoolmate who died. There were always two or three classmates who would pass on every school year. Each time, I would feel very sick and would heave for days on end over the sad and awful news. I am really dismayed to report that not even one "teacher" talked to me, or my classmates, on how to cope when there was a death.

This subject was taboo! I felt that because I was locked in my handicap, none of my teachers knew that I needed to express my emotions. I felt that they didn't care. No one was really that close to me except for my parents, and they suffered right along with me! What I am trying to say is that I believe every school needs to staff a counselor or a psychologist who is trained to give positive support to all children, whether they are handicapped or not.

Of course, before special education classrooms can employ such people, a training program needs to be established. Once when I was given a free TB shot, the nurse thought that I had fainted simply because I dropped my head down, and instantly she reached for the smelling salts. I was, indeed, fortunate to have Mrs. Clark, the aide at Chippendale, by my side to explain to the nurse that I had not fainted—I was just looking away from the needle!

That's why I truly feel that a training program needs to be established for counselors and psychologists, including all who are in the medical field. They need to be educated when they work with the handicapped!!! They must treat us as human beings!

Also, I feel that each physically challenged child must accept his/her affliction and must make the most out of it. I grew up with a very religious mother, who always told me that as soon as I grew up, I would be like anyone else—God was going to grant me a miracle! I didn't understand back then that miracles happen in other ways. I thought that a miracle happened only in a physical sense. However, when it did not occur, I grew quite devastated! I even had suicidal tendencies. This is the only wrong my mother ever did in parenting me. Aside from this, my mother was, and still is, the best mother in the world. Parents and educators must give positive support to help the physically challenged child deal with his/her affliction, to tell them they are beautiful despite their handicaps, and that they can do anything in life if they put their minds to it!

And so my wonderful school years at Chippendale ended. Miss McCall and Mr. Mark were very reluctant when my parents and I decided that I would be going to a new school—named Marjorie F. Carlson. By their sad and disapproving faces, I knew that something was wrong; yet, being so naive, I didn't think that anything was wrong with the school. I just thought that they hated to see me go. After all, I was a good student, who always thirsted for knowledge and was a hard worker. If I knew then what I know now, I would have stayed at Chippendale. But we all make mistakes, and this was mine!

Chapter Four

The Unfortunate Years

I left Chippendale School behind, taking with me many fond memories. It was a school where they had qualified special education teachers. These teachers were devoted to helping their physically challenged students reach their full potential in education. I know that if I hadn't gone to such a fine school I wouldn't be a writer today. I left because I didn't like being the oldest kid in the class, and, at times, I felt extremely lonely. I just wanted to be around kids my own age and have friends. And yet, as it turned out, whether I was around kids my own age or not didn't make any difference. You see, my speech impediment made it, for me, impossible to have friends. People have an extremely difficult time understanding me. This was true whether the people were handicapped or not. I cried a lot back then.

I began Marjorie F. Carlson School in September of 1967, entering the eighth grade. I thought things might be different at Carlson. I've never been able to relate to people, and I know now that that was to be the same whether I was at Chippendale or at Carlson or anywhere else.

My first morning at Carlson was pleasant enough. As always, I was filled with great apprehension and anticipation. When I arrived, I was greeted by a pleasant-looking, stocky, middle-aged man, who was dressed neatly in a suit and tie. He wore horn-rimmed eyeglasses, and to me, he looked like a typical male school teacher ought to look—kind of like "Mr. Novak" in the old television series with James

Franciscus (but not that cute!). His appearance, pleasant manner, and confident attitude impressed me, for he surely reflected intelligence, ability, and integrity. I was later to learn that first impressions can be deceiving.

"Hello," he greeted me. "You must be Loreena Minaudo."

"Yes, I am," I said, smiling as I walked awkwardly with my walker into the school building.

"I'm Mr. C, your teacher, and I've been looking forward to meeting you," he said cheerfully, extending his hand to me. It took me awhile to reach my hand toward his, but he waited patiently as I accomplished my task. We shook hands in greeting.

"Please follow me to my classroom," Mr. C said. We walked slowly until I found myself in a small room, where student desks were arranged circularly rather than in rows.

"This is your desk," Mr. C said, as he pulled out a chair and held it for me while I sat down.

"Thank you." I then waited patiently for class to begin. More students began to filter in, and here and there, I recognized a familiar face from Chippendale. We said hello to each other, and I was beginning to feel more at home.

Distribution of textbooks and practice workbooks, which should be routine at the very onset of any school year, was delayed that day. Unbelievable as it may seem, it took six weeks for these textbooks and workbooks to arrive. During that time nothing academic was taught. We each were told to bring in our own radios and games. Different radio stations could be heard at the same time as we played checkers, Life, or Monopoly games. It seems that our books, without which study, practice, and progress could not be expected, were on order and had yet to be shipped in. If I'd been more audacious, I'd have gone to the principal's office immediately and complained.

Sincerely trying to help me adjust to my new surroundings, Mr. C in fact was overzealous in his promises to me. I felt overjoyed when he told me that he planned to confer with me, review with me, and discuss with me each chapter I would be studying in all my eighth-grade textbooks. It wasn't until I had received my books and workbooks that I found that Mr. C did not give me any direction, correction, or guidance with them. He accepted my typewritten papers and completed worksheets, but he never returned them with corrections or comments.

As time went by, I was convinced that Mr. C's special education classroom wasn't operating as it should. I began noticing such things as classmates listening to radio broadcasts of football or baseball games during class period, indiscriminate use of television sets and movie projectors, and lack of instruction from our teacher. He just sat with his students all day, like a baby-sitter, when, I believe, he should have been teaching. All these wrongs were day in and day out—all day long. Despite these abuses, I gave all of my attention to my schoolbooks. Each day, without exception, I tried hard to acquire a good education by teaching myself.

I remember one day in particular. It was just another ordinary school day in Mr. C's class. I remember hearing the sounds of the radio and TV as I sat at the typewriter. This was my typewriter from home. Carlson did not provide me with one. I classified this as another wrong. Well, anyway, let me continue, shall I? I pretended to have cotton in my ears and ignored the noises as much as possible while trying hard to concentrate on my assignment.

"Going to put these worksheets on Mr. C's desk," Dan, one of my classmates, said as he slowly passed me in his wheelchair.

"Wait, Dan. Will you please take my paper up there too?" I asked.

"Sure."

I smiled as I pushed down the return key on the typewriter, which made the paper slide out. Dan reached and grabbed the sheet of paper from the typewriter and laid it on his lap.

"Thanks," I said, smiling.

"No problem," he said, as he wheeled himself away.

I switched off my typewriter and grabbed onto my walker. My throat felt parched, and I, in a fumbling manner, walked out to the hall and took a drink of water from the drinking fountain. Upon my return, I happened to pass by Mr. C's desk, and I noticed that the drawer was wide open. I thought perhaps he'd forgotten to close it, so I went over and was just about to close the drawer when I noticed that many old worksheets were scattered inside.

These were lessons that I, and some of my classmates, had labored for hours on end to accomplish. They were all unchecked and scattered in the drawer. My chin dropped, and my mouth opened wide. I just stood there with my eyes fixed on the scattered worksheets, completely stunned. Here I was, getting up early, my mother needing to do everything for me so that I could get to school and come away with a good education—and I wasn't learning a damn thing! The "instructor" was doing nothing more than baby-sitting.

There had been so many times when I wondered about my work papers, and here they were—not even one corrected. Feeling like a boiling teapot ready to blow its whistle, I walked back to my desk, where I tried to defuse my anger by getting out a history book and reading it. I sat staring at the book, but I was thinking of what I'd just seen.

Why are my worksheets unchecked? Doesn't Mr. C check them? What does he do all day to earn his pay? Damn it! I wish I was back at Chippendale! Why isn't he educating me? Don't I have a right to a good education? It is my body that is impaired—not my mind. I was starving for intellectual stimulation, and he was denying me the food.

An hour later, when I mustered enough courage, I did approach him and questioned, "Mr. C, how am I doing in my schoolwork?"

He answered, "Oh, just fine, Loreena."

I thought, *How does he know? He hasn't even looked at my papers.*

I asked, in my stumbling voice, "Then may I ask you this? Do you ever check my lesson worksheets?"

The question was a surprise to him, and the expression on his face indicated that he was upset. Nevertheless, Mr. C answered evasively, "I always look them over." Because he was my teacher, I trusted him enough to drop the subject, but in my heart I knew that he was lying.

Until my tenth grade, Mr. C routinely reported to my mother, as well as other mothers of his students, at a parent-teacher conference, the progress of each student. Of course, I was pleased to hear that I was promoted to a grade higher each school year, but I felt little of the satisfaction and the sense of fulfillment that was so often mine following successful progress marked by the completion of my school years as a child at Chippendale. However, my tenth-grade school year ended quite differently. Mr. C decided to issue a final report card to me and to confer with me in lieu of his annual conference with my mother. My conference was strangely irregular, I felt. He began it with a question:

"Loreena," Mr. C asked, "what report card grades would you give yourself if you had to evaluate your own school work?"

You're the teacher; you tell me, I thought to myself, as I swallowed hard. For a few moments, I just sat there. I hardly expected such a question.

"Well?"

"All As, of course!"

"Be serious," Mr. C said, laughing.

I then thought long and hard on it—more than five minutes—and without further hesitation, I recited to him, as if parroting a well-memorized lesson, "Math, B; English, B; History, C; record-keeping, B; social science, C."

I noticed that Mr. C seemed to be recording what I said.

"That's all, Loreena," he stated. "You may go now."

When I got home on the last day of school, I handed my dad my report card.

"Please open it. I want to see my grades."

Dad opened the brown envelope and slid out the report card. He beamed with delight as he looked at the grade markings. He was a short man, five feet, four inches tall and weighed about 160 pounds. His silver gray hair covered a narrow strip around his head. His eyes were hazel, with very long lashes. Anyone who knew my wonderful father would say that he had a dark complexion. But no. My dad was tan only on his arms and face; the rest of his body was just as white and soft as a baby's bottom.

Dad had come to America from Italy when he was twenty-one years old, without a cent to his name and speaking only in his native tongue. He learned how to speak English, and from then on, he worked any kind of a job, from selling Christmas trees to ultimately owning and operating a party store. He loved me and was always proud of me. I was the "apple of his eye." And I idolized my dad so much that, even today, I want to be just like him—a hard worker.

"Let me see," I said.

"You passed, my daughter. You will be an eleventh grader in the fall," he said proudly in his deep Italian accent as he moved the card over to where we both could see it.

Suddenly, my chin dropped and my eyes widened. I turned white as a ghost and beads of sweat formed on my forehead. I sat there, completely stunned, my eyes transfixed on the grade markings. My confused mind drifted back in time to the conference between Mr. C and me.

Staring me right in the face, like some haunted ghost of a dead relative, were the grade markings I had recited to Mr. C.

"What's wrong, Loreena?" Dad asked, as he softly brushed back the hair from my eyes.

I was just about to answer him when my mother walked into the living room. As always, she warmly welcomed me home.

Wearing a smile from ear to ear, Dad quickly got up and showed my mother the report card.

"Oh, wow, you passed!" Mother shouted with glee, as she turned and stooped to kiss me.

I moved back and snarled in anger, "Ma, I told Mr. C those grade markings."

"What?"

"I marked my own report card!" I said and then broke into tears.

"I'm not sure that I understand," Mother said.

Through my bitter tears, I explained. "Mr. C asked me what grade markings I would give myself, and I foolishly told him!"

For a few seconds, they stood in silence. My parents digested the words I had confided to them.

"Loreena, maybe it's a coincidence," Mother said.

"I doubt it."

"Loreena, were you fair when you gave yourself these markings?" Dad asked.

"Yes."

"Well then, don't worry about it. You earned 'em."

"But, Dad, what kind of a teacher is he? He never

teaches! And now he's let us grade our own report cards. He isn't a teacher, but a baby-sitter!" I shouted.

Mother and Father both looked at each other, not knowing what to do. They knew that I wanted a good education, which they both wanted for me, and they knew that Marjorie F. Carlson was the only school around that had a special education room! The implications were that my school was not maintaining responsible standards.

I ended another school year without the desired feeling of fulfillment, for my final report card grades simply could not mean to me symbols of recognized merit as they should. I knew in my own heart that I had worked hard throughout that school year to progress and to achieve in all my subjects, but I felt like my efforts were somewhat unsupported and not fully recognized.

It wasn't until my senior year in Mr. C's class that I heard, through the grapevine, that Mr. C wasn't supposed to be teaching the sixth through twelfth grade. Instead, he was only qualified to teach grade levels one through six. This implication aroused my wrath. I felt as though I had been cheated out of an education. I felt betrayed! I was furious with the principal of Carlson, whom I had never met, and the school board for operating a school like this. A baby-sitter was what they had hired—not a teacher. I was also furious with myself for being so naive. I should have quit school that first year at Carlson and stayed home with a tutor.

I also resented the fact that I had been conscientiously attending high school and had been attentive to the studies given me throughout these years without realizing that I had been receiving an inadequate education.

The buzzer on my oven sounded, it startled me and I jumped, causing my magazine to fly off my lap onto the rug. The opened page—with the article called "Educating Handicapped Children: 10 years of PL 94–142," along with other pages—started to fan until the magazine closed. It reminded me of my school years. Oh, how they have flown by. Such fine and bitter years that needed to be told and then closed—laid by, never to be relived again.

Epilogue

Now that you have read my story, I would like to devote this portion of my manuscript to those readers who are parents of handicapped children, and to offer some suggestions in case you feel your son or daughter is not receiving a proper education.

Today, in the nineties, most handicapped children are being mainstreamed to regular schools, no matter how badly afflicted they are, ensuring these children a proper education. However, if your son or daughter will be entering a special education classroom and is physically and *not* mentally handicapped, then please follow these suggestions:

1. Check out the school.
2. Talk with the principal and the school board about the teachers.
3. Ask for teachers' references.
4. Screen teachers out for yourself and ask many questions.

Once your son or daughter is in a special education classroom, please follow these guidelines:

1. Check for signs of lack of interest in your child and ask him or her why?
2. Discuss with your child what he or she has learned.
3. Keep your eye on your child's homework and check to see if he or she is learning.

4. Give the school about a year. If you feel that your child hasn't learned by then, please, look for another school!

I hope that my story has brought many insights . . . and always remember that a mind must be educated!

About The Author

Four years after my high school graduation, I had such an overwhelming desire for learning that I began taking night courses at a local high school. At first, I tested the waters, so to speak, taking one course at a time. By then, I was twenty-three years old and pretty much knew what I wanted to become—a writer! So the very first class I took was creative writing, followed by an advanced writing class.

At age twenty-six, I began college at Valencia. It is a community college in Orlando, Florida. There, too, I took one course. Back then I think I was too scared, too petrified, and I just wasn't sure that I could do college work due to not having been properly educated in Mr. C's special education classroom. But by being like the little engine that said, "I think I can, I think I can," going up the steep hill, I used positive thinking and surprised myself, receiving an A in the class.

When I returned home from Florida, I quickly enrolled at Macomb Community College in Warren, Michigan, and for the next three years of my life, I took one course per semester.

Due to the illness of my wonderful dad, I had to quit college. It was during this time of my life that I developed my writing skills by writing articles, poems, and children's stories.

In the winter of 1987, I started to write this book. For years, a little voice inside haunted me, urging me to write a manuscript of this nature, and for eons I kept ignoring the voice. But the voice ate and ate through my soul, and I found myself submitting to it.

In the fall of 1988, I reentered Macomb Community College as a part-time student. I do recall that I took English 122, and my first psychology class, Psychology 101.

One semester followed another, and I found my life very hectic. If I wasn't working on my assignments from my devoted college professors, I was working on this manuscript.

While I attended Macomb Community College, I would occasionally have chats with my college "acquaintances," and, being of a curious nature, I would ask them if they had had a good high school education. Their answers were unbelievable! Their first response to my questions, I do believe, was laughter. They all found it hilarious! More than 60 percent of my college "acquaintances," who were mainly able-bodied men and women, said that they were high school dropouts or had had to quit school to get married. Their answers jolted me, and yet they made me feel better about myself. You see, back then I always felt uneducated, even though it was not my fault, it was the school that I attended (Carlson) and the teacher. But I was *not* all that uneducated, nor was I far behind my college classmates. However, there was a little voice inside of me that couldn't help wondering whether, if I had been properly educated back at Carlson, would I have had an associate degree long before 1991? I'll bet my life on it!

While at MCC, I found a few things that bugged the living daylights out of me. I couldn't comprehend that in the 1990s there were, and still are, people who don't know how to push a wheelchair. Here is an example. Pretend you are a new parent and you are outside pushing your neonate in a baby buggy. Suddenly, the front wheels of the baby buggy hit a piece of uneven pavement. You automatically place your foot down on the foot bar and press down slightly, lifting the front wheels, and push it over the uneven pavement. Then you lift up slightly on the handle bar, lifting the back wheels over the uneven pavement. Easy as pie, isn't it? This is exactly how you push a wheelchair!

Another thing that has bugged me to death for eons is that most people think that I am retarded just because I have a speech problem. Even today, I am often talked down to as a child, or ignored. I feel that people need to be educated. But how?

I feel that like a thief in the night my speech impairment has robbed me of friendships. I call my few ex-college classmates "acquaintances" mainly because when we would see each other at college, or even today when I meet some friend at a singles' function, we might greet each other warmly and chat briefly, but they never call to say, "Let's go out for a drink or two. I really would like to get to know you." No, this does not happen, and it's sad!

When I took Psychology 101, the professor taught his students about Erik Erikson's life stages. I grew quite engrossed with Erickson's eight stages of life. However, while I will not write about all eight stages, I must write about the sixth stage.

Erik Erikson's sixth stage, according to *Essentials of Psychology* (1979), by Dennis Coon, is concerned with intimacy versus isolation . . . the need to achieve an essential quality of intimacy in one's life. After establishing a stable identity, a person is prepared to share meaningful love or deep friendship with others. By "intimacy," Erikson means an ability to care about others and to share experiences with them.

In line with Erikson's view, 75 percent of college-age men and women rank a good marriage and family life as their primary adult goal, and yet marriage or sexual involvement is no guarantee that intimacy will prevail. Many adult relationships remain superficial and unfulfilling. Failure to establish intimacy with others leads to a deep sense of isolation. The person feels alone and uncared for in life. This circumstance often sets the stage for later difficulties.

In a sense, I fear this sixth stage. You see, all of my life, due to my handicap and speech impairment, I've been alone. Yes, I have cried rivers. Loneliness is quite painful. Yet, knowing no other life, I have adjusted quite well, I think. I bury myself in my writings, and I read a lot of motivational books to keep my soul alive with positive thoughts! However, on the other hand, I am no different from any other woman. It would be just grand finding that "special" someone.

But I can't help but ponder, after being alone for so many years, *Can I get along with that "special" someone or can't I?* All I know is that once I fell madly in love with a gentleman and had my heart crushed. So, perhaps Erik Erikson's sixth life stage is correct: some people can love and some can't! Either way, I am going to travel steadily down my path of life with or without that "special" someone.

It hasn't been easy—a long, tough road. Yet I feel that during my time at MCC, I ate ravenously of the fruit of the tree of knowledge at my professors' tables and have walked away with a well-taught education.

A very special unforgettable evening for me happened on May 10th, 1991. That night not only did I receive my Associate of Arts degree, but I also received five hundred copies of this book called *A Cry for Education,* which had just been published by Pres. Al Lorenzo at Macomb Community College. And yet, my dream won't be fulfilled until it is circulated all over the United States, for I feel that a book of this nature must become a "teaching guide" for young parents of physically challenged children, special education teachers, and anyone who is interested in knowing what goes on in a special educational classroom.

Yes, my life hasn't been easy. Ever since that cold day on March 3rd, when I fought my way out of my mother's womb, I have fought every inch of the way—struggling with physical and emotional pain. I have no choice—but you, the reader, can choose to make a difference in the lives of people like me.